# ALLEGORIES OF LOVE AND DISASTER

*Brian Brett*

Toronto
*Exile Edition*
1993

This edition is published by Exile Editions Limited, 20
Dale Avenue, Toronto, Canada M4W 1K4. Acknowledge
for assistance toward publication is due the Canada
Council, the Ontario Arts Council, and the Ministry of
Culture, Tourism & Recreation.

Exile Editions Ltd. is distributed in Canada and the
United States by General Publishing, 30 Lesmill Road,
Don Mills, Ontario M3B 2T6.

Designed by Michael P. Callaghan and typeset in
Palatino by Moons of Jupiter, Toronto. Printed and
bound by Best Gagné, Quebec, in December of 1993.

Cover and interior drawings by Claire Weissman Wilks

Author's photo by Cedric J. Barker

ISBN 1-550-96069-5

■ ■ ■

*The Allegories*

## PRELUDE

*It's fixed,*
           *lady.*
*The hunter*
*and his dog*
*will track us*
       *howling*
*into the dirt. . .*

*He will track us by*
*the dust of our throats*
*and the agony of our words.*

*He will track us*
*because we are a cold race*
*and know the ice*
*we meet in our dreams.*

...

All week the snow
has fallen on our shoulders
as if something had died.

Flakes of skin
from a sorcerer's sky.

...

Beginning with a pin prick
of heat in the brain,
a new star exploded.

It fired the creek
in our veins,
our hidden veins.

But even the animals
know their season.
That's what has kept them alive
after the onslaught of us. . .

bundled against the weather,
waiting out the storm.

■ ■ ■

There was lava in our blood.
There was an animal
lost under the sundogs,

There was the perfect, human love waiting
for the never-given sign
that meant an end
to winter's wreckage.

■ ■ ■

Our heads were webbed
by wickedly sentimental visions
of single-masted schooners
and the sea beat of the guitar.

We were going
nowhere very quickly,

and we didn't notice
all the worldly signals;

we refused to acknowledge
the flock of robins
huddled in the poison tree.

...

In this dream
we are alone
in a cold season;
we are walking down the eccentric
road to the disconnected garden.

...

The intelligent animal
cocked his ears
to the new snow,
and moved quietly south,
wet nostrils testing the air,

testing the smell of living death
that seeped through the concrete.

As if he were a ship of flesh
wrecked on land
and searching for a lamp in the storm.

...

The night
painted with a crow's black heart waited outside the window
while we drank wine and listened.

It was our
perfect,
singular,
romantic,
erotic,
somewhat
theatrical
moment:

for two kids
with their noses pressed against
the cool window of the candy shop.

■ ■ ■

After the event
is only deceit.

The sea in the gull's cry
moves the kelp,
and the ship is hooked.

Caught in the net
men and women make,
we listened to the pounding.

...

Yes, there was another man.

You said he was like me
and I was like him.

    We were born to lie;
    a cripple and a runt
    breaking our genes
    on a great thing.

•••

And when you said
that I was a fake
I walked away with a smile.

Believe me;
it's not easy
wearing a wax heart,
candy-wrapped and melting,
behind my teeth.

...

In the dark
the scant, orange leaves
of the wild cherry

wept in the rain.

In the dark of the gut
where bone and tendon
are non-existent
the riverblood was
petrified:
flesh pretending it was rock,
saturated with black wine.

I vomited behind
the scary bushes
because I didn't know
what my body could take.

...

The irrevocable crunch
of the guitar
played against the wall,

The wailing strings
strike their last chord.

Beautiful: the sound
of broken things
inventing harmony.

...

The gaudy guitar
lies broken
among unstrung dreams.

This is the song of two men
    kicked in the throat
      by a beautiful woman.

It passes through centuries
    hand to mouth,
    mouth to mouth,
    hand to hand.

Will we die again?

. . .

This is the turn
where we break
on a sharp stone;

the time
to catch

a thousand birds
with a green net
stretched over the trees.

Never mind
the schooner navigating
the bark of the branches.

Never mind
the wounded oak
dangling its kelpy leaves.

If the catch is too wild
you can

just walk away.

. . .

When the guitar failed
and was thrown to the floor
a lamp faded
far into the ocean.

The gulls cried
and rolled with each wave.

Gull & lamp —
the sea cried.

The kelp moved.
The lovers glanced

at a bird's cold eye.

Love has that ability,
the skill to seek
the ice in the animal.

...

Its strings snapped —
the guitar lay helpless
on its open side.

The gulls faded
against the morning.

The lamp scraped
with the tides
from rock to marine rock.

After the vision
this is what remains:
three lovers and a broken guitar.

Yes, this is what remains
when our history has
seeped into the underground:

$0 + 0 + 0 = 0$

We sink to simple mathematics.

...

Hide yourself, love.
We're going to turn
the world around.

A thick brown nipple
pressed into
the tiny well of the belly.

Somehow, we got
turned around,
the male and female
sockets reversed.

Somehow, we go down,
we go down
to each other,

drunk on the milky secretions,
the sour honey of love
exuding from a human landscape.

...

After I walked away from
your naked music
among the quilts and sheets

I went into the marsh,
high-stepping
through the mud
in a gestapo of desire.

I scared the frogs
and impressed the herons.

I opened my mouth
and tried to drink
all the rain from the sky.

...

Somehow,
        the mad day
was trampled in the mud
on the road to there.

Arrow embedded in rock;
the thought was
a broken shaft,
a puff of slivers
bursting against the air.

And then it came down
like a mediocre rainbow
soaking our skin
with pretty little needles.

We have stolen
the knives of nature
and carved ourselves.

We are tattooed
with an idiot love.

. . .

Is it worth it, these words,
this gathering of energy
like a mountain storm
riding a glaciated peak?

There's so much work
        for a trance
sweet in the body
and hard on the brain.

A variety of sex
that's become a meal
garnished with mixed emotions.

...

Then,
    after dark
    the crow
    donned his cloak of feathers
    and flew into the yellow moon.

...

And there was this man
who touched
a significance
in strange trees,
the wings of little birds,
petrified stones. . .

One
angry
man.

His anger made us
give all that we had to give,
and it was good to give.

Everything that we had.
We gave it away.
I wouldn't have it any other way.

...

The woman is tied to the man
who is tied to the woman
who is tied to the man.

Yes, each is tied
to the veins
of the lovers
sleeping together.

Knot upon knot,
the cords performing
a deranged string game.

■ ■ ■

Over and over again.

After the event
there is only deceit,
the lies we build around our lives.

Over and over again;
the circle takes us around
and then it takes us back again.

...

So we must each have a ship
made of glass
to sail on hell's ocean.

I can see through you.
I know you

and the demons
that haunt
the misguided:

all the ways you will turn,
and you will turn.

Agony of the cutting barnacles,
agony of a tree
spreading its fingers —

a plague of emotions
rises in the glass
vessel,
and we are swamped.

> This I know:
> the anguished look of an old sailor on the
> foundering ship as he sees

> a devil in the masthead.

■ ■ ■

The sea in a gull's cry
moves the kelp
and the ship founders.

    Living in the needle of circumstance
    was a tree of love and fire,

and this is the mad song
of ship and gull and tree.

...

We are a ghostly crew,

all of us naked
to ourselves.

We are
a tree of fools.

    Now in the oak
    was a man.
    The tree shook.
    She smiled.
    He turned his hand
    palm down.
    The other man looked
    at an animal sound.
    The first man
    was angry.
    She cried. They were
    fool and juggler and clown.

...

A trance, a drug,
a spirit
fails us into a sleep
gentle as clouds
that are far away.

Who betrayed who?
I think we betrayed ourselves.

Three suicides
shot with words.

. . .

And the ship scraped its dark belly

on a wild coastline thrown up as a barrier
from inside the groaning planet.

Tree and leaf; the mist lifted
on a welt, a bruise, a scar
carved into the curving bark.

The hands took leaf, and love's
gesture disappeared in the foliage;
but still, love took root
on the blue black mussels.

It took root, and with that glance
the ship turned into a smile.

■ ■ ■

Glorious and cunning,
a light on the mountain
was not only Antares the red star,

but a touch
between man and tree,

as if the cloud were a lamp
caught on the hooked moon.

As if I didn't care.
As if I could prevent

the sea's lift
or a torrent of failures,

the toy glass schooner
that had once sat on the mantle
reflecting in a red storm.

. . .

There was a hunter
playing in the snow,

his dog lost,
wired on every scent
they encountered.

It couldn't figure out
the smell of words,
or the way we make sense
out of senselessness.

And the hunter
died in the snow
because he was afraid
of everything, of dogs
and dreams that suck
us down with that trick
of cold which makes
even dying seen warm.

...

All the ways I could love
caught in a drowning lamp.

I need you
like the moon needs to full.

And the gull cries.
And the kelp moves.

And the ship sinks.
And the moon falls down.

...

In a dream I saw
a wingshot crow
which did not know
how to fly,
even as it flew.

Then I saw an old man
climbing the mast
to relight the lamp,

the cold wind
sinking into his ribs.

...

He has fed all the gulls
and still they feed.

This is the way of the world.
There's never enough to eat.
Even when your belly is full.

...

The drowning frigate
in a last attempt
at independence
threw its bow
into the stars;
then sank,

the rudder
tangled
in the jewelled seaweed.

The mast
carried sails
of bright kelp.

> You don't know
> what it means
> to look down
> and find only
> water between your legs.

...

The impression of a storm
flung its shadow
across the mountains.

And after the storm
what passes then?

A gesture of friendship
thrown into the moving ocean
dances across the waves.

What happens to the old frigate
when the swinging lamp
finally snaps out?

A sea of clouds
rises above the western horizon,
and a squall of white birds
swamps the moon.

I wonder
where will I be
when the real,
aging vessel
drifts silently
to sea bottom —

the shattered lamp
weeping gasoline on dark water?

. . .

Through the night window
I can see nothing.

It is cold outside.
The dog is howling,
but ship and storm and gull
have followed the tree
into nowhere and the night.

Ink on paper is
all that's left,
a few lives
crumbling to slow
decay and dust. . .
the painted
paper crow
hanging over my desk.

...

I remember you,
    lady,
I remember you
with oak leaves, the product
of an ancient tree.

I remember you,
with torment and ecstacy,
I remember you
under naked stars. . .
all that we have done.

I remember your pain.
I remember your nipples,
the mad and scary
way you sang when we made love.

I remember the sinking ship called
a relationship between juvenile delinquents.

...

The dog that followed me
everywhere I went
and lay beside the bed
where we made love,

even she has gone
down the channels
into a different zone.

■ ■ ■

The dog that followed me
everywhere I went,
and lay beside all
the beds of love,

is the dog I murdered.
I killed her the day
she couldn't get off the floor.

My sweet dog. My love.
Now your ashes sit on my desk
because I don't know
where to bury you.

■ ■ ■

We will make an accounting,
bookkeepers of our lives.

We will number what we have
and what we have lost.

And I will take what I can see;
the catalogue of leftovers
from the adventure
called forty years in the world.

What do they mean?
Nothing.

What are they?
Nothing.

Each one full of power,
like the romances I once lived
with ships and trees and gulls
and absurd, broken guitars.

...

We thought we were the generation
that was going to change the planet.

We thought we were unique
with our ships and dogs,
our guitars and our dreams.

But our machine was more deadly
than anything else that has passed
over the razed ground.

We are just chimpanzees in a lab
where the man in the white coat
has gone permanently to lunch.

...

I might be an aging man
in an old room.

I might be like you.
I might be you.

That's alright, we can
sing together.

We can sing together.
We can invent new ways
out of old dreams.

We can be unabashed,
romantic and sentimental.
All that's wrong with those words
is our attitude towards them.

Like everything in this world,
they are only evil when we become
their victims. Victims, especially
the broken ones, are also evil.

That's right, dance.
Dance until you are dead.

● ● ●

The allegories of love and disaster,
the code words
the signals, the lights,
the dreams, and the tawdry
remnants of failed actions.

These are my gifts to myself.
I'd name them for you,
but the names have no meaning;
fish hooks and ancient sculptures,
dead dogs and stuffed crocodiles
relate only to their owners.

And the dream I want to tell
is somehow outside
of the objects it has collected.

...

Alright, the gestures
in a woman's face.

They play havoc
with every man's history.

I could catalogue your eyebrows,
your mouth, and your hands.
I could sing all the keys
that your voice contains.

But time and paper
have seen too many
centuries of such attempts.

So I just walk away from my desk,
buckle my coat against the snow,
and kiss our history goodbye.

•••

Like the broken guitar
              we are
made to resemble
what we once were.

The clock strikes.
The snow falls.
The ghost of an animal
        turns over,
reliving in its sleep
the moment when it was awake.

The rifle is stuffed
in a closet somewhere,
and the hunter long gone.

It's time to carry time in our hands.
Time to throw one more look
                over our shoulders.

It's time to glance again in the mirror
            at a shivering reflection
            before it fades into reality.

The long, downward slide
of aging bodies
has caught up with me.

I must have
winter on my mind.

Brian Brett is the author of several books of prose and poetry, including: *Fossil Ground At Phantom Creek; Smoke Without Exit; Evolution In Every Direction; The Fungus Garden; Tanganyika;* and *Poems, New And Selected.* He has just completed his latest novel, *Coyote.* The author lives with his family on Salt Spring Island, where he cultivates his garden and creates ceramic forms.